STOCKING STUMPERS

SPORTS
2014

By S. Claus

RED-LETTER PRESS, INC.
Saddle River, New Jersey

Red-Letter Press, Inc.
P.O. Box 393, Saddle River, NJ 07458
www.Red-LetterPress.com
info@Red-LetterPress.com

ACKNOWLEDGMENTS
SANTA'S SUBORDINATE CLAUSES

Compiled By:
Steve Fiorentine

Editor:
Jack Kreismer

Contributor:
Jeff Kreismer

Cover & Page Design:
Cliff Behum

Special Mention:
Sparky Anderson Kreismer

INTRODUCTION

Whether you're having a few quiet
moments to yourself or enjoying a
reunion with friends and family, Stocking
Stumpers is the perfect holiday companion.
Gather 'round the Christmas tree or simply
kick back in your easy chair while
trying out the holiday humdingers,
tailor-made tests and trivia tidbits.

Once you've had a sampling, I think you'll
agree, Stocking Stumpers is proof of the
Christmas pudding that good things do
come in small packages. Ho ho ho!

Merry Christmas!!

S. Claus

The Mantle Meter

'Tis right around Christmas
and all through the book,

There are all sorts of stumpers
everywhere that you look.

There are quizzes and seasonal tests
to take you to task,

But what are those "stocking"
questions you ask?

Well, the stockings are hung
by the chimney with care.

The more that are filled,
the tougher the bear.

And so it is that
the Mantle Meter keeps score,

Rating the stumpers,
one stocking or more.

STOCKING
STUMPERS

SPORTS
2014

FAMOUS 14s

See if you can identify the following
players who wore the jersey number 14.

1. This six-time NBA champion was
voted MVP in 1957 after leading the
league with 7.5 assists per game.

2. In 1982, this player became the first
quarterback to pass for 4,000
yards in three straight seasons.

3. Despite having 4,256 career
hits, this player is not in the
National Baseball Hall of Fame.

4. This player is Major League
Baseball's all-time leader in games played
without making a postseason appearance.

5. In 1963, this player became the first
quarterback to throw over 30
touchdown passes in consecutive seasons.

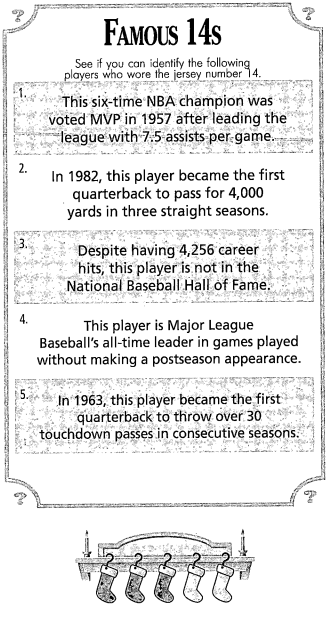

Super Bowl XLIX is set to be played on
February 1, 2015, at what venue?

ANSWERS

1.

Bob Cousy

2.

Dan Fouts

3.

Pete Rose

4.

Ernie Banks

5.

Y.A. Tittle

University of Phoenix Stadium

GRAYBEARDS

1. In 2014, what goalkeeper became the oldest player to ever play in a World Cup when he took the field against Japan at 43 years old?

2. With 67, at the age of 42 in 2013-14, what New Jersey Devil became the oldest NHL player to lead his team in points in over 40 years?

3. With a solo shot against the Twins on July 2, 2014, who became the oldest player in Kansas City Royals history to hit a home run at 42 years of age?

4. Who is the oldest coach to win a Super Bowl?

5. A year after becoming the oldest player in MLB history to hit a walk off home run, who was baseball's oldest active player in 2014 at 43 years of age?

Who did Peyton Manning throw his record-breaking 51st touchdown pass of 2013 to?

ANSWERS

1.

Faryd Mondragon (Colombia)

2.

Jaromir Jagr

3.

Raul Ibanez

4.

Tom Coughlin, 65

5.

Jason Giambi

Julius Thomas

MISCELLANEOUS MINDBENDERS

1. Players had to deal with what inconvenience during Game 1 of the 2014 NBA Finals?

2. For the first time in 2014, honorary captains drafted teams for the Pro Bowl. What Hall of Famers served as the first-ever captains?

3. In 2014, who became the first American male runner to win the Boston Marathon since 1983, posting a time of 2:08:37?

4. Richard Sherman defeated what player in the finals of the *Madden NFL 15* Cover Vote?

5. True or False: The NBA's new Charlotte Hornets absorbed the history and records of the original Hornets franchise from 1988-2002.

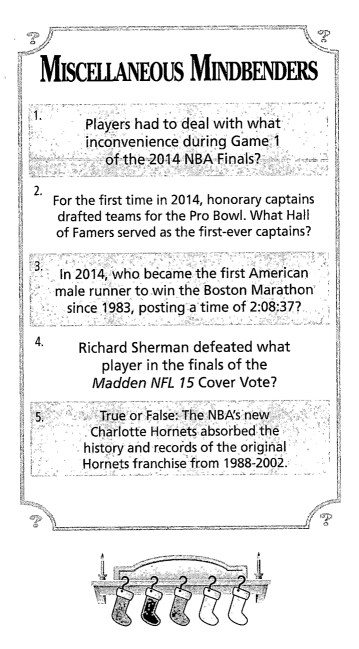

Derek Jeter hit a home run off of what Cy Young Award-winning pitcher for his milestone 3,000th hit?

ANSWERS

1.

The AT&T Center's air conditioning malfunctioned.

2.

Jerry Rice and Deion Sanders

3.

Meb Keflezighi

4.

Cam Newton

5.

True

David Price

Booked

The following players all got coal in their stockings in 2014.

1. Uruguay's Luis Suarez was handed a nine game international match ban by FIFA for biting what Italian defender during the teams' Group D World Cup matchup?

2. After leading the NFL in receiving yards in 2013, what wide receiver was suspended the entire 2014 season for a failed drug test?

3. What pitcher was suspended 10 games in 2014 for being caught with pine tar on his neck during a game against the Boston Red Sox?

4. This player missed the 2014 Stanley Cup Finals after being suspended 10 games for using physical force against a linesman during the Eastern Conference Finals.

5. After an appeal, it was ruled that Alex Rodriguez would be suspended for the entire 2014 season. How long was MLB's original punishment?

 # ❄ SEASONAL STUMPER ❄

Born on Christmas Day 1946, this five-time Pro Bowl fullback was named the MVP of Super Bowl VIII. Can you name him?

ANSWERS

1.

Giorgio Chiellini

2.

Josh Gordon

3.

Michael Pineda

4.

Daniel Carcillo

5.

211 games

Seasonal Stumper Answer:

Larry Csonka

ODD MAN OUT

1. Which player was not a member of both the Los Angeles Kings 2012 and 2014 Stanley Cup-winning teams: Marion Gaborik, Jonathan Quick or Mike Richards?

2. Which of the following players did not take part in the 2014 Home Run Derby: Nelson Cruz, Todd Frazier or Justin Morneau?

3. Which of the following San Antonio Spurs players has not won an NBA Finals MVP award: Manu Ginobili, Kawhi Leonard or Tony Parker?

4. Which of the following venues has not hosted a Super Bowl: Ford Field, LP Field or Lucas Oil Stadium?

5. Which of the following players was not a first round selection in the 2014 NBA Draft: Doug McDermott, Shabazz Napier or Glenn Robinson III?

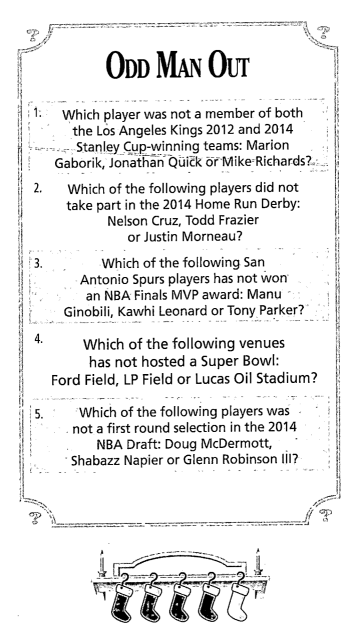

What Basketball Hall of Famer pitched a shutout for the Chicago White Sox on August 13, 1963?

ANSWERS

1.

Gaborik

2.

Cruz

3.

Ginobili

4.

LP Field

5.

Robinson III

Dave DeBusschere

Baseball Bafflers

1. In April of 2014, what player burst onto the scene by setting rookie records with 10 homers and 31 RBIs?

2. Tim Lincecum threw his second career no-hitter on June 25, 2014. Against which team has Lincecum tossed both of his no-no's?

3. On April 22, 2014, who became the first player in MLB history to hit career home runs number 499 and 500 during the same game?

4. By no-hitting the Rockies on June 18, 2014, who became the only player in MLB history to strike out 15 batters in a game without allowing a hit or a walk?

5. Before losing to the Chicago Cubs on May 20, 2014, Masahiro Tanaka had not been defeated in how many consecutive starts between Japan and the majors?

The Houston Astros failed to sign what player they drafted with the #1 overall pick in the 2014 First-Year Player Draft?

ANSWERS

1.

Jose Abreu

2.

San Diego Padres

3.

Albert Pujols

4.

Clayton Kershaw

5.

42

Brady Aiken

FORMERLY KNOWN AS...

Uncover the former names of the following ballparks.

1.

   ## Minute Maid Park

2.

   ## The Rogers Centre

3.

   ## Progressive Field

4.

   ## Chase Field

5.

   ## AT&T Park

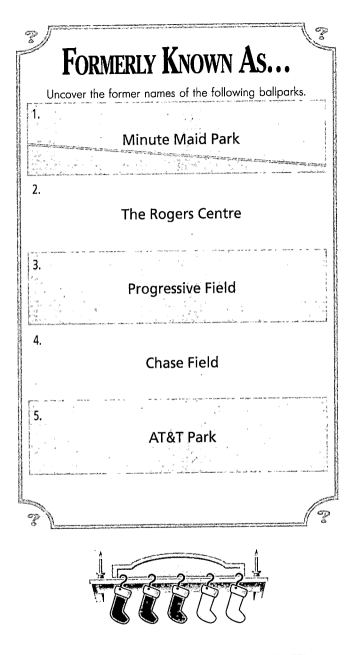

What player was named MVP of Super Bowl XLVIII?

ANSWERS

1.
Enron Field (Houston)

2.
SkyDome (Toronto)

3.
Jacobs Field (Cleveland)

4.
Bank One Ballpark (Arizona)

5.
Pacific Bell Park or SBC Park
(San Francisco)

Seattle's Malcolm Smith

GOOOAAALLLLLL

1. On July 1, 2014, what goalkeeper set the record for most saves in a World Cup match with 16 stops against Belgium?

2. In the 95th minute against the United States, what Portuguese player scored the latest regulation goal in World Cup group-stage history?

3. With his 16th career goal against Brazil in the semi-finals, who became the World Cup's all-time leading scorer in 2014?

4. Who won the Golden Boot as the World Cup's top scorer with six goals during the 2014 tournament?

5. Germany's rout of host nation Brazil in the semi-finals was the largest winning margin ever in a World Cup final or semi-final. What was the final score?

❄ SEASONAL STUMPER ❄

Five Golden Rings... Only one NFL player has been a member of five Super Bowl championship teams- two in San Francisco and three in Dallas. He also shares his first name with the author of *A Christmas Carol*. Name him.

ANSWERS

1.

Tim Howard (USA)

2.

Silvestre Varela

3.

Miroslav Klose (Germany)

4.

James Rodriguez (Colombia)

5.

7-1

Seasonal Stumper Answer:

Charles Haley

"B" ROLL

Each of these answers have last names
that begin with the letter B.

1.

On May 25, 2014, who tossed a no-hitter
against the Philadelphia Phillies in which he
walked three batters and struck out six?

2.

As a member of the Spurs in 2014,
who became the first Italian-born
player to win an NBA championship?

3.

What player took home the
Selke Trophy in 2014 for being the
NHL's best defensive forward?

4.

What player was named the captain
of the American League squad for the
2014 Home Run Derby at Target Field?

5.

In Super Bowl XLVIII, this player led
all Seahawks receivers with five
receptions for 66 yards to go along
with a touchdown. Who is he?

What two hockey players tied for the lead in scoring at
the 2014 Sochi Winter Olympics with five goals apiece?

ANSWERS

1.

Josh Beckett

2.

Marco Belinelli

3.

Patrice Bergeron

4.

Jose Bautista

5.

Doug Baldwin

Michael Grabner (Austria) and
Phil Kessel (United States)

UNIFORMITY

Match the players in each column who wear
the same uniform number as each other.

1. Carmelo Anthony   a. Dale Earnhardt, Jr.

2. Robinson Cano   b. Colin Kaepernick

3. Jamaal Charles   c. Joey Logano

4. Patrick Kane   d. Mark Teixeira

5. Russell Wilson   e. Dwyane Wade

Who won the Best Young Player award
at the 2014 FIFA World Cup?

ANSWERS

1.
b (7)

2.
c (22)

3.
d (25)

4.
a (88)

5.
e (3)

Paul Pogba (France)

LOOK WHO'S 50!

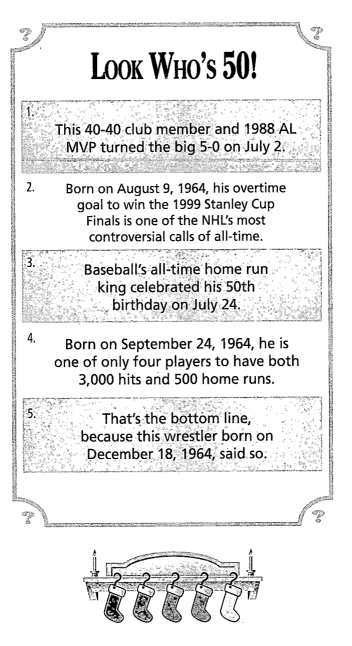

1. This 40-40 club member and 1988 AL MVP turned the big 5-0 on July 2.

2. Born on August 9, 1964, his overtime goal to win the 1999 Stanley Cup Finals is one of the NHL's most controversial calls of all-time.

3. Baseball's all-time home run king celebrated his 50th birthday on July 24.

4. Born on September 24, 1964, he is one of only four players to have both 3,000 hits and 500 home runs.

5. That's the bottom line, because this wrestler born on December 18, 1964, said so.

With a home run in 45 different ballparks, what player holds the major league record for venues homered in?

ANSWERS

1.

Jose Canseco

2.

Brett Hull

3.

Barry Bonds

4.

Rafael Palmeiro

5.

"Stone Cold" Steve Austin

Sammy Sosa

EITHER OR

1. Which quarterback threw for more yards in Super Bowl XLVIII: Peyton Manning or Russell Wilson?

2. Which center averaged more rebounds during the 2013-14 NBA season: Andre Drummond or DeAndre Jordan?

3. Which early-exiting country had more wins in the 2014 FIFA World Cup: England or Italy?

4. Which center scored more points during the 2013-14 NHL season: Ryan Getzlaf or Claude Giroux?

5. Which wide receiver was drafted earlier in the 2014 NFL Draft: Mike Evans or Sammy Watkins?

❄ SEASONAL STUMPER ❄

In 1923, President Calvin Coolidge lit the first National Christmas Tree, the same year in which what iconic venue, home to 100 World Series games, opened its gates for the first time?

ANSWERS

1.

Manning (280 yards)

2.

Jordan (13.6 rebounds per game)

3.

Italy (one win)

4.

Getzlaf (86 points)

5.

Sammy Watkins

Seasonal Stumper Answer:

Yankee Stadium

LETTER PERFECT

1. What Miami Marlins catcher has the longest last name in Major League Baseball history?

2. Do you know the four NBA team nicknames that do not end in the letter "s"?

3. Name the only NFL team whose nickname starts with a vowel.

4. Who are the two NHL teams whose city and nickname start with the same letter?

5. In 2014, the Tampa Bay Rays wore a patch on their uniform sleeve with the letters ZIM in memory of what longtime baseball figure?

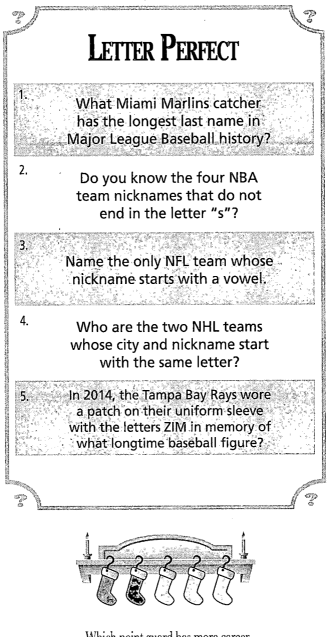

Which point guard has more career steals: Jason Kidd or Gary Payton?

ANSWERS

1.
Jarrod Saltalamacchia

2.
Miami Heat, Orlando Magic,
Utah Jazz and OKC Thunder

3.
Philadelphia Eagles

4.
Boston Bruins and
Pittsburgh Penguins

5.
Don Zimmer

Kidd (2,684)

SECOND GUESSING

1. In 2014, who became just the second player to win back-to-back Home Run Derby titles?

2. With his second career Norris Trophy in 2013-14, who became the only active defender to win the award multiple times?

3. Who became the just the second rookie in MLB history to hit seven home runs over a seven-game span in 2014?

4. The United States of America finished second to what country in the medal count for the 2014 Sochi Winter Olympics?

5. Mike Trout became the second-youngest player to win All-Star Game MVP honors in 2014 at Target Field. Who is the youngest player to win the award?

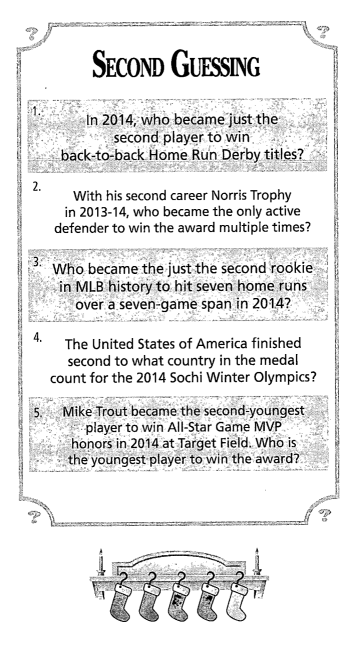

What former NHL player was a contestant on season 18 of *Dancing with the Stars* in 2014?

ANSWERS

1.

Yoenis Cespedes

2.

Duncan Keith

3.

George Springer

4.

Russia

5.

Ken Griffey, Jr. (1992)

Sean Avery

IT'S ABOUT TIME

1.
From the end of the previous play,
how long is the play clock in the NFL?

2.
In soccer, how long is each
extra time period?

3.
What race is known as "The
Fastest Two Minutes in Sports"?

4.
Who was on the pole for the 2014
Daytona 500 by recording the fastest time
in qualifying with a 45.914 second run?

5.
In 2014, who logged the longest
home run trot ever recorded in Major
League Baseball at 32.91 seconds?

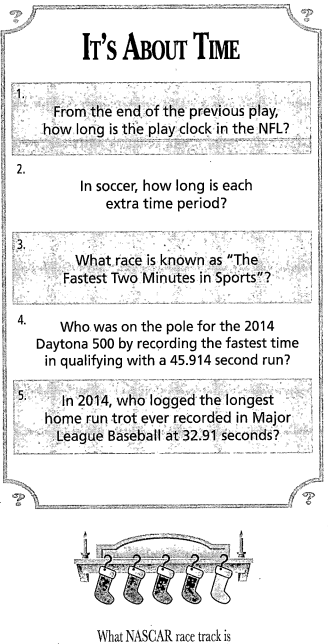

What NASCAR race track is
nicknamed "The Lady in Black"?

ANSWERS

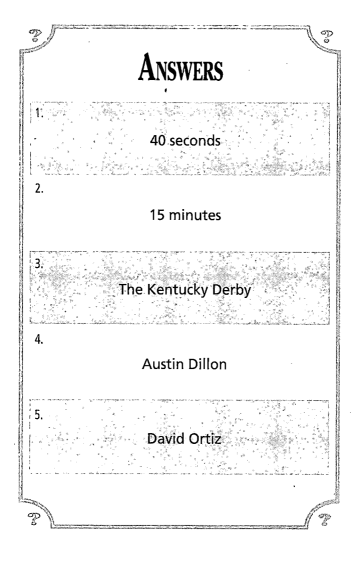

1.

40 seconds

2.

15 minutes

3.

The Kentucky Derby

4.

Austin Dillon

5.

David Ortiz

Darlington Raceway

Seeing Double, Initially

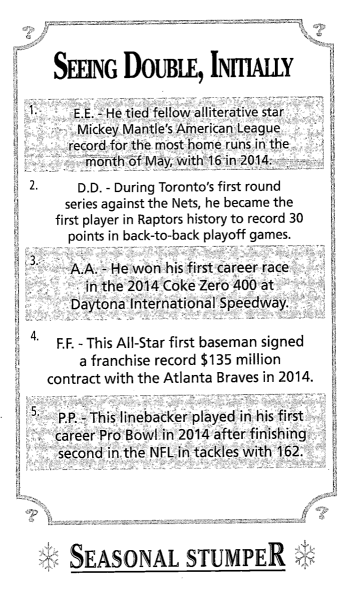

1. E.E. - He tied fellow alliterative star Mickey Mantle's American League record for the most home runs in the month of May, with 16 in 2014.

2. D.D. - During Toronto's first round series against the Nets, he became the first player in Raptors history to record 30 points in back-to-back playoff games.

3. A.A. - He won his first career race in the 2014 Coke Zero 400 at Daytona International Speedway.

4. F.F. - This All-Star first baseman signed a franchise record $135 million contract with the Atlanta Braves in 2014.

5. P.P. - This linebacker played in his first career Pro Bowl in 2014 after finishing second in the NFL in tackles with 162.

❄ Seasonal Stumper ❄

In the 2003 holiday film *Elf*, lead character Michael wears what New York Jets player's #80 jersey?

ANSWERS

1.

Edwin Encarnacion

2.

DeMar DeRozan

3.

Aric Almirola

4.

Freddie Freeman

5.

Paul Posluszny

Seasonal Stumper Answer:

Wayne Chrebet

GOING, GOING, GONE

The following sports figures said farewell in 2014.

1. With 684 goals, who retired in 2014 as the 11th-highest scorer and highest-scoring Finn in NHL history?

2. What 14-time Pro Bowler retired in 2014 holding the NFL records for most touchdowns and receiving yards by a tight end?

3. After calling it quits on his 13-year NBA career in 2014, what five-time champion was immediately hired as the head coach of the New York Knicks?

4. After assuming office in 1998, his tenure as commissioner of Major League Baseball came to an end in 2014. Who is he?

5. In February of 2014, Adam Silver succeeded this man as NBA commissioner. Can you came him?

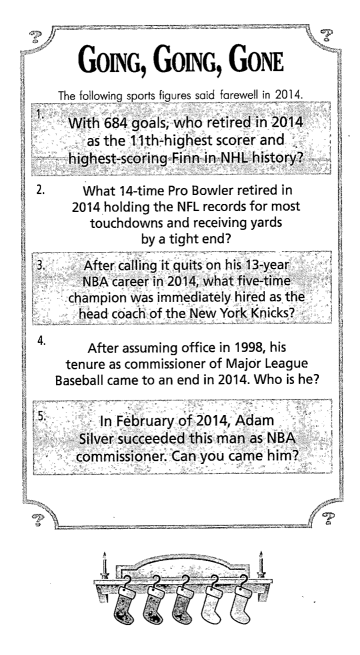

In bowling, how many strikes equal a turkey?

ANSWERS

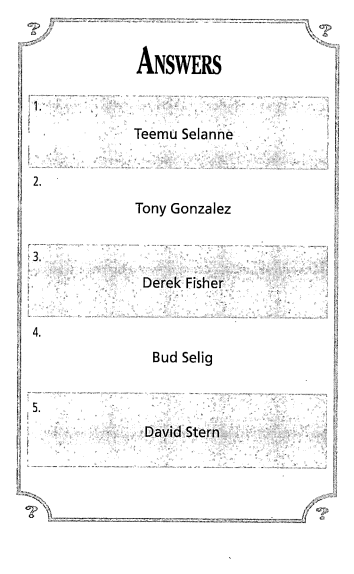

1. Teemu Selanne

2. Tony Gonzalez

3. Derek Fisher

4. Bud Selig

5. David Stern

Three

DYNAMIC DUOS

1. On July 13, 2014, what pitcher-catcher combo became the first pair of batterymates to hit grand slams in the same game?

2. What pair of teammates finished first and second in three pointers made in the 2013-14 NBA season?

3. In front of the hometown fans, what Twins pitcher-catcher duo came in for the ninth inning of the 2014 MLB All-Star Game at Target Field?

4. Who were the only two players to score a hat trick during the 2014 FIFA World Cup?

5. What pair of #1 draft picks are the only two Canadian-born players to be selected first overall in the NBA Draft?

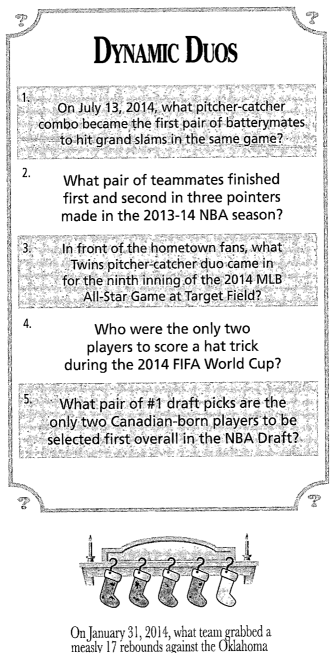

On January 31, 2014, what team grabbed a measly 17 rebounds against the Oklahoma City Thunder, an NBA all-time low?

ANSWERS

1.

San Francisco's
Madison Bumgarner and Buster Posey

2.

Golden State's Stephen Curry
(261) and Klay Thompson (223)

3.

Glen Perkins and Kurt Suzuki

4.

Thomas Muller (Germany) and
Xherdan Shaqiri (Switzerland)

5.

Anthony Bennett (2013) and
Andrew Wiggins (2014)

Brooklyn Nets

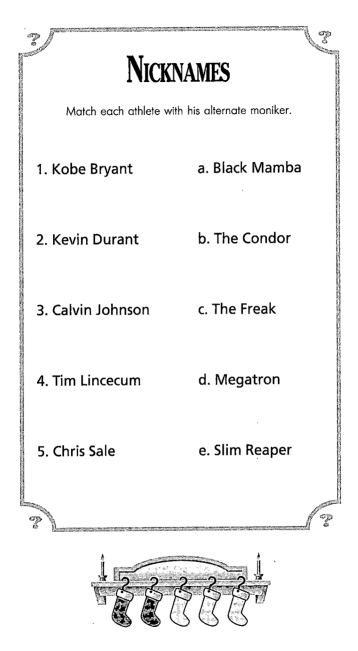

NICKNAMES

Match each athlete with his alternate moniker.

1. Kobe Bryant   a. Black Mamba

2. Kevin Durant   b. The Condor

3. Calvin Johnson   c. The Freak

4. Tim Lincecum   d. Megatron

5. Chris Sale   e. Slim Reaper

True or False? The 2013 Denver Broncos are the only team in NFL history to score more than 600 points in a season.

ANSWERS

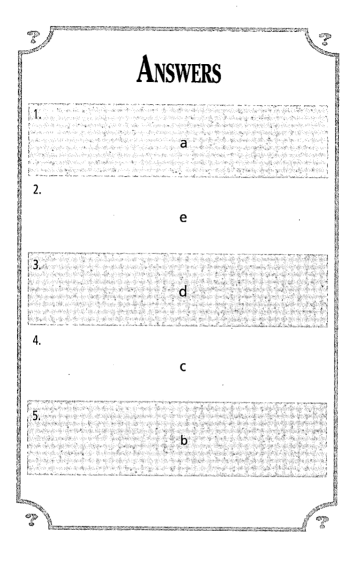

1.

                    a

2.

                    e

3.

                    d

4.

                    c

5.

                    b

True

HARDCOURT HODGEPODGE

1. In how many consecutive games did Kevin Durant score 25 points during the 2013-14 NBA season, marking the third longest streak in league history?

2. The Thunder and Grizzlies set an NBA playoff record in 2014 when they played how many straight overtime games during their first round matchup?

3. True or False: The 2013-14 season marked the first time in NBA history that the Celtics, Knicks and Lakers all failed to make the playoffs in the same season.

4. On December 3, 2013, what two players became the first rookies to record their first career triple-doubles in the same game?

5. The Philadelphia 76ers tied an NBA record for futility when they lost how many straight games during the 2013-14 NBA season?

❄ SEASONAL STUMPER ❄

Fact or Fib: The town of Christmas was once the spring training home of the Minnesota Twins.

ANSWERS

1.

41

2.

Four

3.

True

4.

Victor Oladipo and
Michael Carter-Williams

5.

26

Seasonal Stumper Answer:

Fib- But there really is a Christmas, Florida, halfway
between Cocoa and Orlando in Orange County.

THE CAPTAIN

Derek Jeter's storied career with the Yankees came to a close in 2014. Santa salutes him with this true or false quiz.

1.

T or F: Derek Jeter is the only player to record 3,000 hits in a Yankees uniform.

2.

T or F: No one has played more career games at shortstop in major league history than Jeter.

3.

T or F: Jeter has played in more postseason games than any player in major league history.

4.

T or F: In 2000, Jeter became the only player in major league history to win the All-Star Game MVP and World Series MVP awards in the same season.

5.

T or F: No player has received more All-Star votes in their career than Jeter.

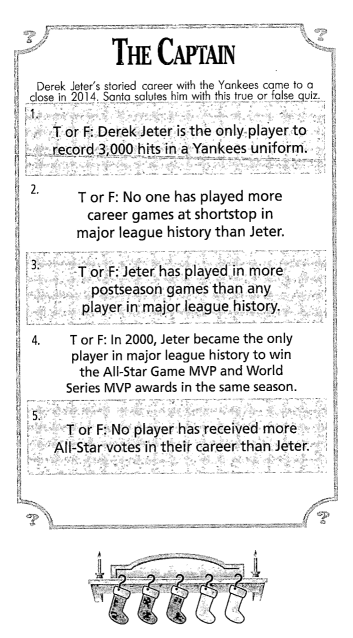

Super Bowl-winning quarterback Russell Wilson was acquired by what team in MLB's 2013 Rule 5 Draft?

ANSWERS

1.

True

2.

False- Omar Vizquel holds the record
with 2,709 games player at short.

3.

True

4.

True

5.

False- Jeter is second to Ken Griffey,
Jr., who owns 50,045,065 votes.

Texas Rangers

UNDER THE SEA

1. Who finished second in AL MVP voting to Miguel Cabrera in each of his first two major league seasons?

2. What relief pitcher was nicknamed "El Pulpo," Spanish for octopus, because he had six fingers on each hand?

3. Who are the only two MLB franchise that have not hosted the All-Star Game?

4. By going 17-0 in 1972, who is the only NFL team to win the Super Bowl with a perfect season?

5. With a 1.46 mark, what pitcher nicknamed "The Shark" set a major league record for lowest ERA by a winless pitcher through his first 10 starts in 2014?

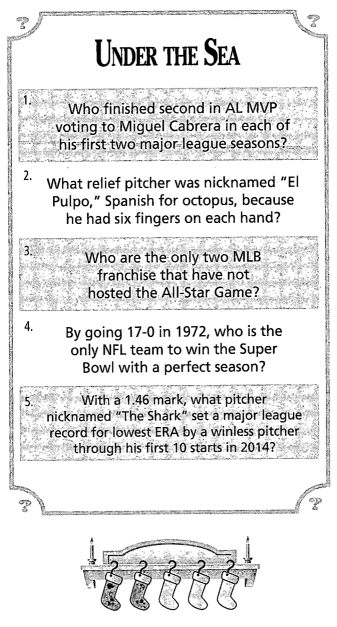

For the first time since 1997, what player was not in the Colorado Rockies 2014 Opening Day lineup after retiring in the offseason?

ANSWERS

1.

Mike Trout

2.

Antonio Alfonseca

3.

Miami Marlins and Tampa Bay Rays

4.

Miami Dolphins

5.

Jeff Samardzija

Todd Helton

PIGSKIN PICK'EMS

Which Hall of Famer...

1.
Has more career sacks:
John Randle or Michael Strahan?

2.
Passed for more career yards:
Warren Moon or Fran Tarkenton?

3.
Had more career touchdown
receptions: Cris Carter or Steve Largent?

4.
Returned more interceptions for
touchdowns in his career:
Aeneas Williams or Rod Woodson?

5.
Started more playoff games:
John Elway or Joe Montana?

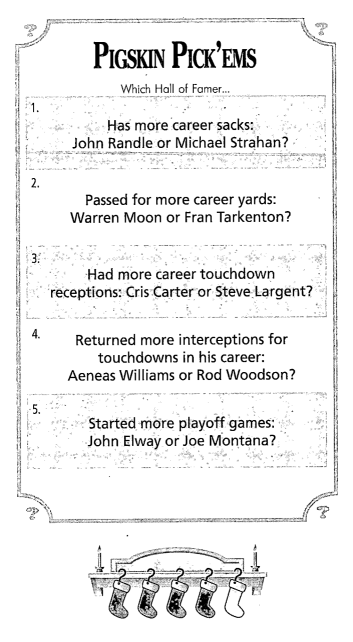

What player holds the NFL record for most
receiving yards in a single playoffs with 546?

ANSWERS

1. Strahan (141.5)

2. Moon (49,325)

3. Carter (130)

4. Woodson (12)

5. Montana (23)

Larry Fitzgerald, in 2008

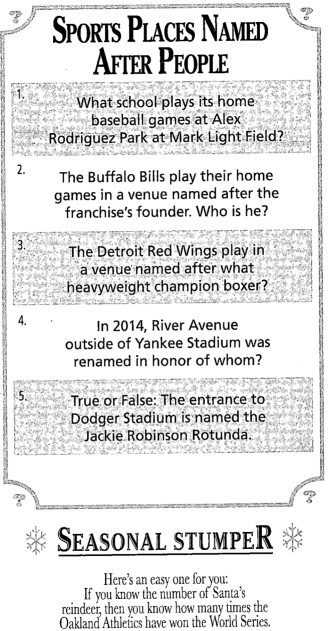

SPORTS PLACES NAMED AFTER PEOPLE

1. What school plays its home baseball games at Alex Rodriguez Park at Mark Light Field?

2. The Buffalo Bills play their home games in a venue named after the franchise's founder. Who is he?

3. The Detroit Red Wings play in a venue named after what heavyweight champion boxer?

4. In 2014, River Avenue outside of Yankee Stadium was renamed in honor of whom?

5. True or False: The entrance to Dodger Stadium is named the Jackie Robinson Rotunda.

❄ SEASONAL STUMPER ❄

Here's an easy one for you:
If you know the number of Santa's reindeer, then you know how many times the Oakland Athletics have won the World Series.

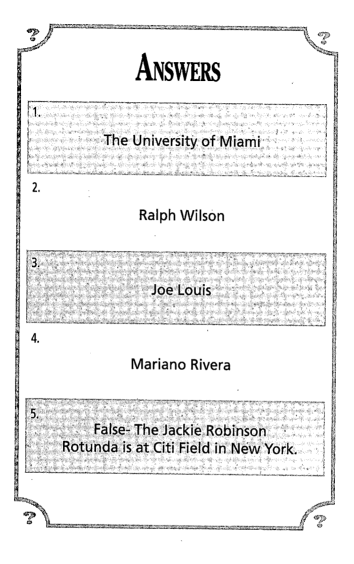

ANSWERS

1.

The University of Miami

2.

Ralph Wilson

3.

Joe Louis

4.

Mariano Rivera

5.

False- The Jackie Robinson
Rotunda is at Citi Field in New York.

Seasonal Stumper Answer:

9

(If you thought 8, maybe you
forgot to add Rudolph to the others.)

MEASURING UP

1.
How far is the pitcher's mound from home plate on a major league baseball diamond?

2.
What has an arc radius of 23 feet, 9 inches?

3.
In 2013, what kicker set the NFL record for longest field goal by booting a 64-yarder?

4.
Which league's playing surface is 200 feet long and 85 feet wide?

5.
Which major league ballpark is home to the deepest centerfield in the majors at 436 feet?

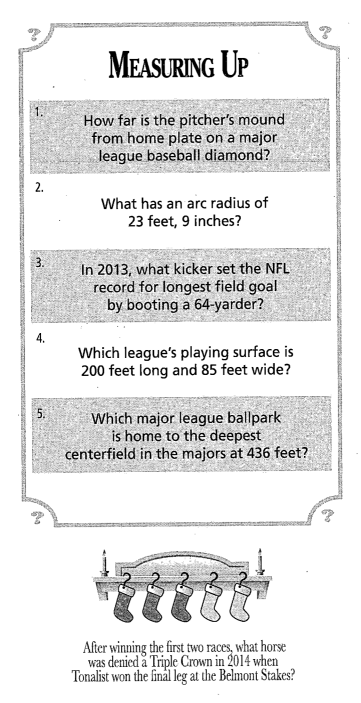

After winning the first two races, what horse was denied a Triple Crown in 2014 when Tonalist won the final leg at the Belmont Stakes?

ANSWERS

1.

60 feet, 6 inches

2.

The NBA three-point line

3.

Matt Prater

4.

NHL

5.

Minute Maid Park

California Chrome

SLAP SHOTS

1. What NHL award is given annually to the player who leads the league in total points at the end of the regular season?

2. Who took home the Vezina Trophy in 2014 as the league's best goaltender?

3. On October 3, 2013, what Boston Bruin became the first player in NHL history to score his team's first goal of the season on a penalty shot?

4. Who was the MVP of the 2014 NHL All-Star Game?

5. Who scored the only goal of the Olympic semi-final game between the United States and Canada in Sochi?

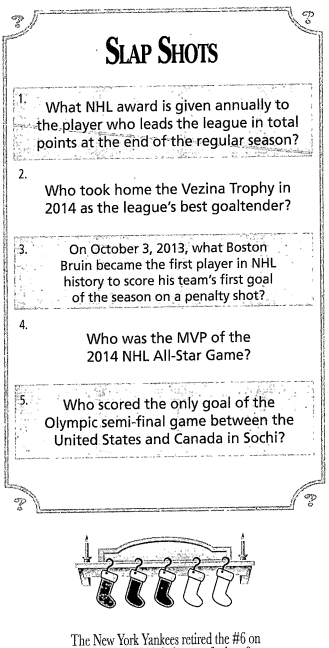

The New York Yankees retired the #6 on August 23, 2014, in honor of whom?

ANSWERS

1.

Art Ross Trophy

2.

Tuukka Rask

3.

Chris Kelly

4.

No one- There was no All-Star
Game due to the Olympics.

5.

Jamie Benn (Canada won.)

Joe Torre

100 YEARS AGO

1. On July 11, 1914, this pitcher made his first career major league start for the Boston Red Sox. Can you name him?

2. Now the second-oldest park in all of baseball, this venue opened its gates for the first time on April 23, 1914. Can you name it?

3. Nicknamed "The Yankee Clipper," this future Hall of Famer was born on November 25, 2014. Do you know him?

4. The 1914 World Series marked the first time in Fall Classic history that a four-game sweep occurred. What team handled the Philadelphia Athletics?

5. What broadcaster, who'd become famous for singing "Take Me Out to the Ball Game," was born on March 1, 1914?

What two gofers share the record for the most consecutive years winning at least one PGA tournament, with 17?

ANSWERS

1.

Babe Ruth

2.

Wrigley Field

3.

Joe DiMaggio

4.

Boston Braves

5.

Harry Caray

Jack Nicklaus and Arnold Palmer

WHO AM I?

1. After being drafted by the Cleveland Browns with the 22nd pick, my jersey became the highest-selling in the NFL before I ever played a game.

2. At 19 years and 342 days old, I am the youngest player to ever win the Heisman Trophy.

3. After the 2013 NFC Championship Game, Richard Sherman called me a "sorry receiver" during a post game tirade.

4. I lived up to my nickname of "Mr. Game 7" in winning the Conn Smythe Trophy as the Stanley Cup Playoff MVP in 2014.

5. I set a U.S. Open record for the lowest score after two rounds by shooting a 130 on my way to winning at Pinehurst in 2014.

❄ SEASONAL STUMPER ❄

What two NFL teams traditionally play on Thanksgiving every year?

ANSWERS

1.

Johnny Manziel

2.

Jameis Winston

3.

Michael Crabtree

4.

Justin Williams

5.

Martin Kaymer

Seasonal Stumper Answer:

Detroit Lions and Dallas Cowboys

TRIPLE PLAY

1. After the trade deadline in 2014, the Detroit Tigers pitching rotation consisted of the three most recent AL Cy Young Award winners. Can you name them?

2. In total, how many NBA titles did the Miami Heat's "Big Three" of LeBron James, Dwyane Wade and Chris Bosh win?

3. Who is the only player to be voted the NFL's MVP three years in a row?

4. What three players were first ballot National Baseball Hall of Fame inductees in 2014?

5. Who are the only three players in Major League Baseball history to hit a home run before turning 20 and after turning 40?

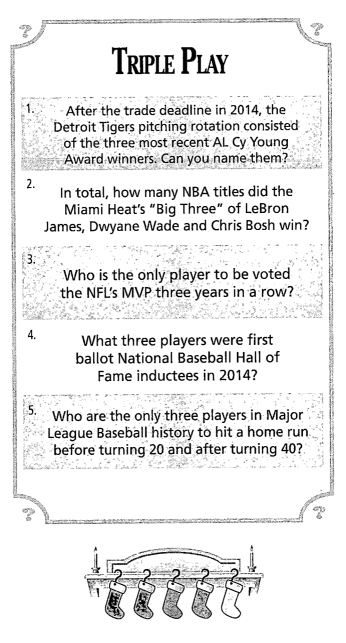

Beginning in 2015, what Major League Soccer team will call Yankee Stadium home?

ANSWERS

1.

Justin Verlander (2011), David Price (2012) and Max Scherzer (2013)

2.

Two

3.

Brett Favre (1995-97)

4.

Tom Glavine,
Greg Maddux and Frank Thomas

5.

Ty Cobb, Gary Sheffield and Rusty Staub

New York City FC

ON POINT

Match the following point guards to
the colleges they attended.

1. Kyrie Irving   a. Duke

2. Chris Paul   b. Kentucky

3. Derrick Rose   c. Memphis

4. John Wall   d. UCLA

5. Russell Westbrook   e. Wake Forest

What seven-time NBA champion earned
the nickname "Big Shot Rob"?

ANSWERS

1.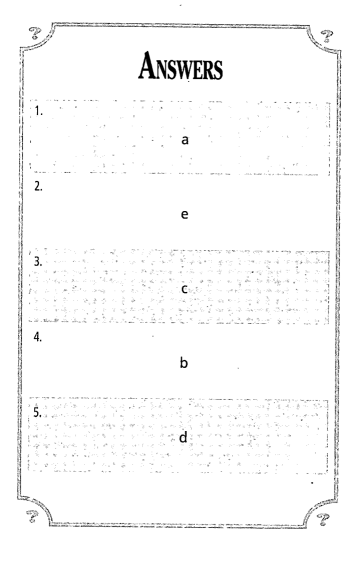

   a

2.

   e

3.

   c

4.

   b

5.

   d

Robert Horry

OLYMPIC SITES

Match each city to the year in which it hosted the Olympic games.

1. Beijing   a. 2006

2. London   b. 2008

3. Sochi   c. 2010

4. Turin   d. 2012

5. Vancouver   e. 2014

To celebrate its 50th anniversary in 1996, the NBA released a list of its greatest 50 players to ever play the game. Which was the last to retire?

ANSWERS

1.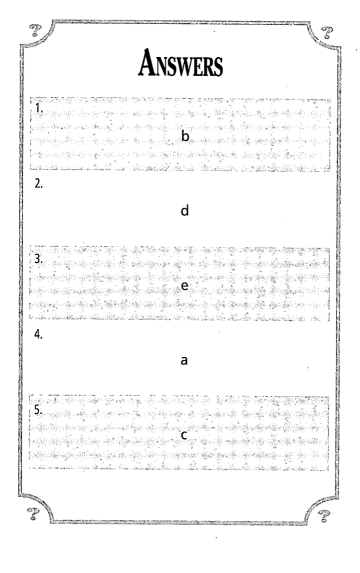

    b

2.

    d

3.

    e

4.

    a

5.

    c

Shaquille O'Neal, in 2011

ROLE PLAYERS

1. What baseball player appeared as a bartender in the 2013 film *Dallas Buyers Club*?

2. Who portrayed Muhammad Ali in the 2001 biopic *Ali*?

3. What major league team does 11-year-old Billy Heywood inherit in the 1994 movie *Little Big League*?

4. What 1977 film follows a minor league hockey team named the Charleston Chiefs?

5. The 2014 movie *Draft Day* follows the fictional general manager of what NFL franchise?

❄ SEASONAL STUMPER ❄

In 1984, what New York Knicks player set the record for most points scored in a single Christmas Day game by dropping 60 on the New Jersey Nets?

ANSWERS

1. Adam Dunn

2. Will Smith

3. Minnesota Twins

4. *Slap Shot*

5. Cleveland Browns

Seasonal Stumper Answer:

Bernard King

FANTASTIC FOUR

Each of the following involve
championships in a year ending in "four."

1. The 1984 NBA Finals was the first of three title meetings between Magic Johnson's Lakers and Larry Bird's Celtics. Which team was victorious the first time around?

2. What Stanley Cup-winning defenseman was named the 1994 Conn Smythe winner as the MVP of the playoffs?

3. The 1964 NFL Championship was the last professional sports title for what city?

4. The Red Sox four-game sweep of the St. Louis Cardinals in the 2004 World Series ended a title drought of how many years for Boston?

5. Who won the 1994 World Series?

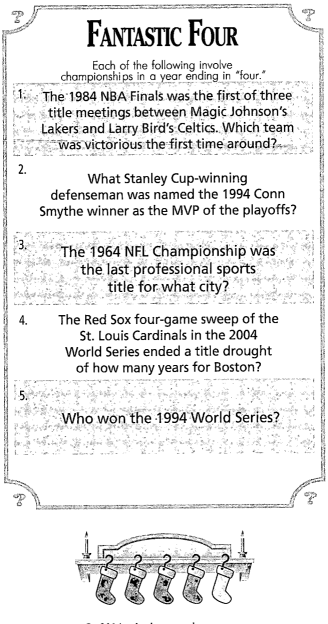

In 2014, who became the youngest player in NHL history to win the Calder Memorial Trophy as the Rookie of the Year?

ANSWERS

1.

Celtics

2.

Brian Leetch

3.

Cleveland

4.

86

5.

No one- It was cancelled due
to the player's strike.

Nathan MacKinnon

COACHING CAROUSEL

Match the Super Bowl-winning
coaches with their teams.

1. Pete Carroll   a. Baltimore Colts

2. Tom Coughlin   b. San Francisco 49ers

3. Tom Flores   c. New York Giants

4. Don McCafferty   d. Oakland/L.A. Raiders

5. George Seifert   e. Seattle Seahawks

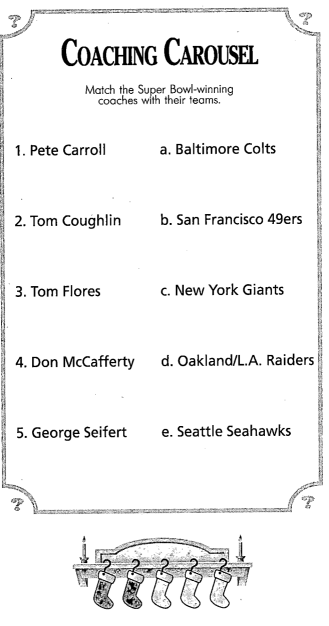

True or False? #7 Connecticut became
the lowest-seeded team to win the NCAA
men's basketball tournament in 2014.

ANSWERS

1.

  e

2.

  c

3.

  d

4.

  a

5.

  b

False- Villanova won it as an eight-seed in 1985.

PRESIDENTIAL

Each of these answers contains a U.S. President's last name.

1. For the first time since 1997, the Yankees and Red Sox made a trade with each other on July 31, 2014. The BoSox sent Stephen Drew to the Bombers for what player?

2. After being released by the Philadelphia Eagles, this Pro Bowl receiver moved on to the rival Washington Redskins. Can you name him?

3. After playing five different positions for the Pittsburgh Pirates, what utility player was named to his first All-Star team in 2014?

4. The Green Bay Packers selected what safety out of the University of Alabama with the 21st overall pick in the 2014 NFL Draft?

5. Who was selected the 2014 NBA Rookie of the Year while playing with the Philadelphia 76ers?

In 1990, what 42 to 1 underdog defeated Mike Tyson for the Heavyweight Championship, thus putting an end to Tyson's unblemished record?

ANSWERS

1.

Kelly Johnson

2.

DeSean Jackson

3.

Josh Harrison

4.

Ha Ha Clinton-Dix

5.

Michael Carter-Williams

Buster Douglas

THE ONE AND ONLY

1. In 2014, who became the only substitute in World Cup history to score a game-winning goal in the final?

2. Who is the only player in NBA history to win a championship in three different decades as a starting player?

3. Only one player in the video game *Madden NFL 15* is featured with his authentic tattoos. Can you name him?

4. In 2014, who became the only pitcher in Major League Baseball history to make 14 straight starts allowing two runs or fewer while pitching at least seven innings?

5. On January 1, 2014, who became the only player in NFL history to win five MVP awards?

❄ SEASONAL STUMPER ❄

True or False: Santa dons a red jacket for his Christmas Eve sleigh ride every year as does the winner of The Masters on the Sunday of the first full week of April every year.

ANSWERS

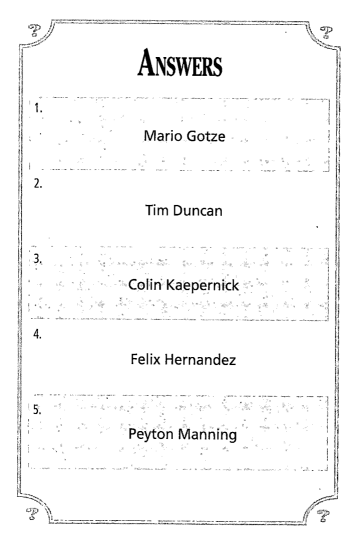

1.

Mario Gotze

2.

Tim Duncan

3.

Colin Kaepernick

4.

Felix Hernandez

5.

Peyton Manning

Seasonal Stumper Answer:

False- The green jacket is awarded to the winner.

THE AGONY OF DEFEAT

1. Who joined the Phillies and Braves in 2014 as the only MLB teams to lose 10,000 games in their history?

2. What Cardinals baserunner was picked off by Boston's Koji Uehara to end Game 4 of the 2013 World Series, marking the first time a postseason game ended on a pickoff?

3. What team blew a 28-point lead and ended up losing to the Indianapolis Colts in the 2013 AFC Wild Card Game?

4. Despite losing in the final, who was awarded the Golden Ball as the World Cup's best player in 2014?

5. Who is baseball's all-time leader in losses, with 316 defeats?

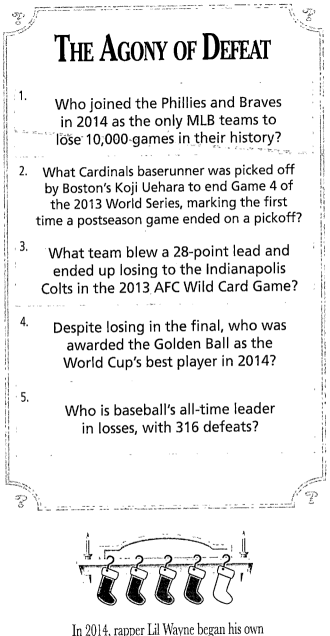

In 2014, rapper Lil Wayne began his own sports management company. Who was the first athlete to sign with Weezy?

ANSWERS

1.

Chicago Cubs

2.

Kolten Wong

3.

Kansas City Chiefs

4.

Argentina's Lionel Messi

5.

Cy Young (He also won the
most games, 511.)

Cristiano Ronaldo

GLOBAL GAME

1. The 2014 MLB All-Star Game at Minnesota's Target Field featured five Cuban-born All-Stars. Can you name them?

2. True or False: Germany's victory at the 2014 FIFA World Cup in Brazil was the first time a European country won the tournament in Latin America.

3. Which of the following NBA MVPs did not play for Team USA at the 2014 FIBA Basketball World Cup in Spain: Kevin Durant, LeBron James or Derrick Rose?

4. The NFL played a record how many games in London during the 2014 season?

5. Who was the captain of Canada's gold medal-winning ice hockey team at the 2014 Sochi Winter Olympics?

Which of the following players did not win the NL Rookie of the Year Award: Chris Coghlan, Khalil Greene or Jason Jennings?

ANSWERS

1.

Jose Abreu, Yoenis Cespedes,
Aroldis Chapman, Yasiel Puig
and Alexei Ramirez

2.

True

3.

James

4.

Three

5.

Sidney Crosby

Greene

Animal Kingdom

1.
What 2012 gold medal gymnast is known as "The Flying Squirrel"?

2.
What animal nickname is the most commonly-used in all of college sports?

3.
What two-time All-Star third baseman and World Series MVP goes by the nickname "Kung Fu Panda"?

4.
What NFL team's group of fans is referred to as the "Dawg Pound"?

5.
Can you name all five NFL teams named after birds?

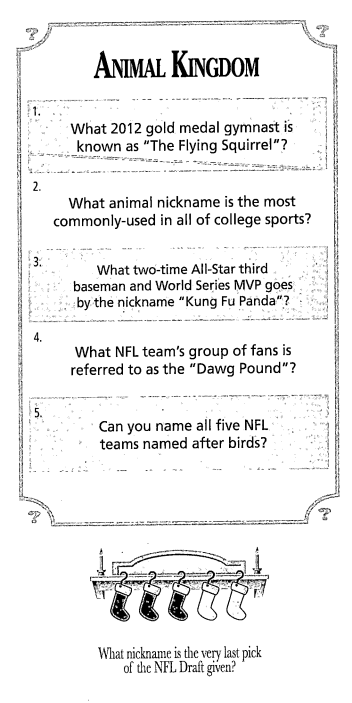

What nickname is the very last pick of the NFL Draft given?

ANSWERS

1. Gabby Douglas

2. Eagles

3. Pablo Sandoval

4. Cleveland Browns

5. Cardinals, Falcons, Ravens, Eagles and Seahawks

"Mr. Irrelevant"

QB QUIZ

Match the following quarterbacks to
the colleges they attended.

1. Drew Brees   a. Auburn

2. Andrew Luck   b. California

3. Eli Manning   c. Mississippi

4. Cam Newton   d. Purdue

5. Aaron Rodgers   e. Stanford

❄ SEASONAL STUMPER ❄

This second baseman was born on December 25,
1927, and grew up to become a 19-year big
leaguer. He made 15 All-Star teams and was named
the AL's MVP in 1959. Can you name him?

ANSWERS

1.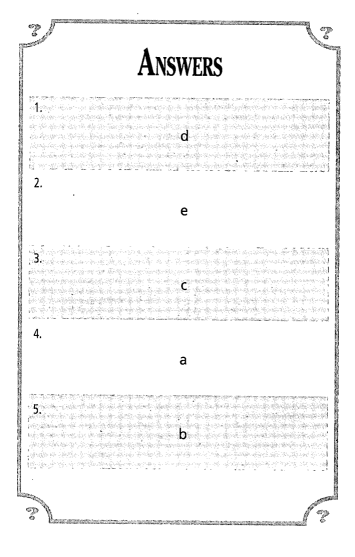

   d

2. e

3. c

4. a

5. b

Seasonal Stumper Answer:

Nellie Fox

VOWEL PLAY

Their first and last names are in order, but the vowels have been removed. See if you can identify these current stars.

1.

JKMNH

2.

JHNTVRS

3.

DMNLLLRD

4.

JSBTST

5.

GNCRLSTNTN

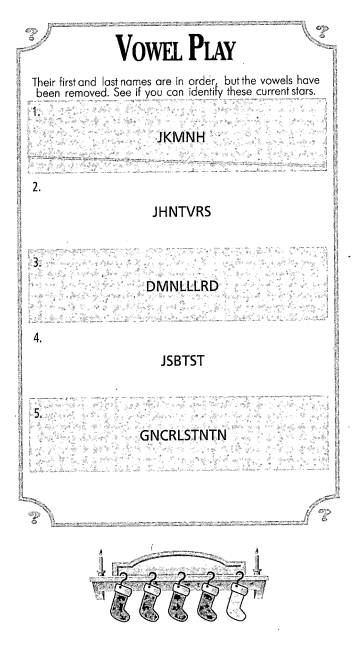

Who was the first Wild Card team to win a Super Bowl?

ANSWERS

1.

Joakim Noah

2.

John Tavares

3.

Damian Lillard

4.

Jose Bautista

5.

Giancarlo Stanton

Oakland Raiders (Super Bowl XV)

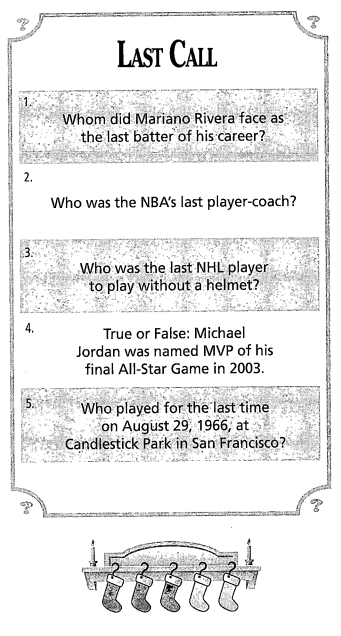

LAST CALL

1. Whom did Mariano Rivera face as the last batter of his career?

2. Who was the NBA's last player-coach?

3. Who was the last NHL player to play without a helmet?

4. True or False: Michael Jordan was named MVP of his final All-Star Game in 2003.

5. Who played for the last time on August 29, 1966, at Candlestick Park in San Francisco?

In 2014, what player became the fastest pitcher in MLB history to reach 500 career strikeouts?

ANSWERS

1.

Yunel Escobar

2.

Dave Cowens (1978-79)

3.

Craig MacTavish

4.

False- Kevin Garnett was.

5. The Beatles- Some Christmas trickery from Santa to close things out- It was their final live concert... Merry Christmas!

Yu Darivsh